P9-DDP-992

Brain Builders

...NOT!

by
Lisa Eisenberg and Katy Hall

SCHOLASTIC INC.
New York Toronto London Auckland Sydney

*To Annie Eisenberg
and
Charlie Kleuser*

No part of this publication may be reproduced in whole or in part, or stored in a retrieval system, or transmitted in any form or by any means, electronic, mechanical, photocopying, recording, or otherwise, without written permission of the publisher. For information regarding permission, write to Scholastic Inc., 730 Broadway, New York, NY 10003.

ISBN 0-590-47295-X

12 11 10 9 8 7 6 5 4 3 2   3 4 5 6 7 8/9

Printed in the U.S.A   01

First Scholastic printing, November 1993

● ● ● ● ● ● ● ● ● ● ● ● ● ●

You know who they are. They're the kids who actually like math. They're the kids who actually believe study hall is for studying—instead of for throwing spitballs and snoozing. They're the kids who always remind the teacher when he forgets to give a test. They're the kids who can't get enough of those brain-building books that promise to challenge your I.Q., expand your mental power, and test your creativity.

● ● ● ● ● ● ● ● ● ● ● ● ● ● ●

But, hold it. What about the other kids? The great-looking, popular, C+ average, terrific kids? Kids (like you?) who only enjoy solving problems such as how many times can you chew a piece of gum before sticking it on the bottom of your seat in the movie theater and starting in on the popcorn? Or just how many calls you can make to the 1(900) JOKE LINE before your mom freaks out when she gets the phone bill? Where is the book for *you*?

● ● ● ● ● ● ● ● ● ● ● ● ●

Well, up until last Thursday, that book was nowhere. It didn't exist. But then— WHAMO! Out of nowhere it appeared!

Welcome to the wacky world of...

Brain Builders
...NOT!

Contents

....

Not *continents*, Contents!
Like, what's in this book?

Contents

....

Psst! You know none of this contents bologna is going to be in this book, right?

CONGRATULATIONS!

You're getting smarter already!
Your I.Q. just went up 4 points!

Now sharpen two #2 pencils, sit up straight at your desk, and get ready...get set...go.

No, no! We didn't mean go away! We meant get ready to go to work. Sheesh!

Subtract those 4 points.

Now, before you begin, you will need to fill out our registration form. If you are accepted as one of our select students, then and only then will you be eligible to participate in:

Brain Builders
...NOT!

We need the facts...just the facts.

Brain Builders Registration

Directions

Read each question. Think about what it says. If you haven't got anything better to do, answer it.

Identification

1. What is your full name?

_____

2. What is your half name?

_____

3. What do you wish your name was?

_____

4. Does anyone ever call you Foofoo?

_____

5. Do you ever answer to this name?

_____

6. Why did you purchase this book?

_____

7. Are you sorry?

_____

8. How sorry?
    Sort of _____ Pretty _____
    Very _____Totally _____

Vital Statistics

1. Height when wearing your mother's high heels _____

2. Weight when holding your dog _____

3. Eye color:
Left _____ Right _____ Center _____

4. Hair color:
Monday _____ Wednesday _____
Friday _____

5. Nail Color:
Right Pinkie _____ Left Thumb _____

6. Teeth: Yep_____ Nope_____

7. Nose: (check all that apply)
Big _____ Teensy _____ Broken _____
Tilted _____ Snoutlike _____
Drippy _____ Stuffy _____

Mental State

California_____ Alaska_____

Rhode Island_____ Arkansas_____

Creativity

1. If you were a musical instrument, would you be a...?
   Tuba _____ Kettle Drum _____
   Triangle _____ Flute _____
   Big Mac _____

2. If you were a vegetable, would you be a...?
   Rutabaga _____ Snap Bean _____
   Chickpea _____ Horseradish _____
   Side of Fries _____

3. If you were a nut, would you be a...?
   Filbert _____ Pecan _____
   Coconut _____ Cashew _____
   Bless You _____

4. If you were to write a book, the title would probably be...

Brain Surgery in Five Easy Lessons _____

I Was a Fifth-Grade Belly Dancer _____

Swamp Thing From the Boys' Room _____

Counting on Your Fingers Can Be Fun _____

5. If you were to star in a film, it would most likely be...

The Mummy _____

My Friend Flicka _____

Night of the Living Dead _____

Home Alone, Part XXXVII _____

6. If you have free time, you most like to spend it by...

Running around the mall like a maniac _____

Listening to *Hooked on Phonics* _____

Watching *Mr. Rogers' Neighborhood* _____

Dressing up like Mr. Rogers _____

What? You actually finished filling out the registration form? You're in worse shape than we suspected. Much worse. You need the immediate help of a qualified Mental Engineer.

Fortunately for you, we have just completed our M.E. First Degrees, so we can say, without reservation, that we will not be able to have a table ready for you until the ten P.M. seating.

And that's way past your bedtime.

Hints on Scoring Well on the Battery of Brain Builders

•••

1. Get a lot of sleep—but not *while* you're taking the tests!

2. Eat a confidence-building breakfast. Here is our suggested menu:

> 1/2 grapefruit
>
> 1 cup cooked oatmeal
>
> 1 teaspoon brown sugar
>
> 1/2 cup low-fat milk
>
> 2 strips lean bacon
>
> 1 fried egg
>
> 2 slices whole wheat toast

Put all ingredients into a blender. Puree at high speed for up to sixty seconds, longer if the grapefruit rind is tough or the raw bacon gets wrapped around the blender blades. Pour the result into a tall glass and drink it down.

IF YOU CAN DO THIS,
YOU CAN DO ANYTHING!

3. Do not study. No amount of last-minute cramming on state capitals or how to convert centigrade to a better grade will help. (Don't you wish your teachers would say this sometimes?)

4. Do not send a chimpanzee to take the tests for you. In the past five years, chimps have done particularly well on these tests and have thrown off the results. Guinea pigs, gerbils, or other members of the rodent family are acceptable substitutes.

5. Should you guess? Not unless you want to. Then go ahead. Or maybe you shouldn't. We don't know. What do you think?

Brain Facts

Before you begin taking the tests that will boost your intelligence, you should know something about how the human brain works. (If you have recently had a chicken brain transplanted into your skull cavity, skip ahead to page 85.)

This is a diagram of the normal human brain:

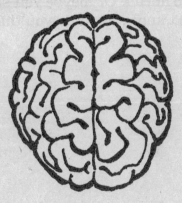

On this page is a diagram of the brain of the first human to complete the whole course of

Brain Builders
...NOT!

As you can see, certain areas of the brain have become overdeveloped. This person is now the mental equivalent of Arnold Schwarzenegger. But BEWARE! In order to keep this mental muscle, the student *must* reread *Brain Builders...NOT!* at least five times a day. If you are not up to this kind of rigorous mental schedule, or you think your mother will burn this book if she sees your nose stuck in it even one more time, then *do not even begin.*

WE WARN YOU, DO NOT CONTINUE, OR YOUR BRAIN, TOO, WILL START TO DEVELOP.

WE WILL NOT, WE REPEAT, *NOT*, BE RESPONSIBLE FOR THE RESULTS!

I.Q. Pre-test

....

Okay, you risk-taker, you. Decided to plunge ahead into the unknown lands of higher intelligence, eh? Well, don't say we didn't warn you.

Directions

Answer these three questions. By analyzing your responses, amazingly enough, we will determine your *exact* I.Q.

1. Which of the following scientific formulas best describes the weight of gravity on a day in which the humidity is fourteen percent?

(a) Only $13.95, but hurry! Sale ends Saturday!

(b) U R A Q T I N V U

(c) Similac

2. The meaning of the word *vidaspecificaspatially* is defined as:

(a) an ancient term for a jar of pickles

(b) a really long word with lots of letters

(c) like a really cute word to use to impress your boyfriend's parents

3. What number can be doubled, resulting in an even number, tripled, resulting in an odd number, and quadrupled, resulting in a number so odd that no one has ever heard of it?

(a) 6

(b) six

(c) Could you repeat the question?

I.Q. Pre-test Analysis

Answers

1. The correct answer is (d). Yes, this answer was omitted from your answer sheet. Highly intelligent students, of course, grasp this immediately, and simply write in the answer.

2. Again, the correct answer is (d). The third letter in the word *vidaspecificaspatially* was your clue.

3. Here, the correct answer is, what else, (d). The number is 2,354,873,672,981.

I.Q. Scoring

You can score this test yourself by carefully following these directions:

EXAMPLE:

1. Total the number of correct points you scored on the test.

0

2. Multiply by your shoe size.

$0 \times 10\frac{1}{2} D = 0$

3. Divide by the number of toes on your left foot.

$0 \div 6 = 0$

4. Multiply by your teacher's age.

$0 \times 51 = 0$

5. Divide by the age your teacher claims to be.

$0 \div 21 = 0$

6. The result is your I.Q.:

0

Brain Builder...Not! Tests

Coming Right Up
Here We Go
Alley-Oop!

Before you begin, carefully look over this checklist to see if you are *really* ready:

_____ Have you visited the restroom?

_____ Are your two #2 pencils sharpened so that their points will snap the second they touch the paper?

_____ Do you know where a pencil sharpener is located in the testing room?

_____ Have you set your VCR to tape the episode of *I Dream of Jeannie* that you'll be missing while you take these tests?

If you can honestly answer "Yes!" to each of these questions, then you may BEGIN!

$$\frac{1}{2} = .50$$

$$.035 = 3.5\%$$

$$.95 = 95\%$$

: Math
: Section

$$50\% \text{ of } 39 =$$

$$3a + 2b = 1c$$

$$\begin{array}{r} 34 \\ 96 \\ 87 \\ +26 \\ \hline \end{array}$$

$$37°F =$$

If Sally Ann
has six mice to
feed to her
boa constrictor...

$$E = mc^2$$

Word Problems

You all know how to do these little math blasters. So...hurry up and do 'em; we don't have all day.

1. If you have fifteen friends over for dinner and you have only twelve apples, how can you divide the apples so that everyone gets the same amount to eat?

___ (a) cut each apple into fifteen pieces

___ (b) make applesauce

___ (c) feed the apples to the dog and send out for pizza

2. If you and *three* friends attend a rock concert given by *Six* Feet Under and you buy *four* hot dogs for *one* dollar each out of your *five*-dollar bill, what is the name of the warm-up group?

___ (a) *Three* Blind Mice

___ (b) *Two* for Tea

___ (c) Snow White and the *Seven* Dwarfs

3. You've saved the coupons from dog food packages for three years now and you're ready to go shopping. If each coupon is good for 3 cents off on each separate purchase of a $5.95 bag of Kanine Kibbles, and you have 678 coupons, how long will your dog have to live to eat all the food you are going to buy him?

____ (a) forever

____ (b) seven light years

____ (c) what's got a dog?

4. If you are lying in your bed at night and you hear three loud knocks, followed by seven low whistles, followed by nineteen spine-chilling howls, and, after forty-two seconds of silence, a pair of bloodcurdling screams, you can be sure that right outside your window is:

____ (a) someone with a calculator to count all these stupid noises

____ (b) a few representatives of The Living Dead

____ (c) all your friends having a party that they didn't invite you to

5. Ella is three years older than Tom. Tom is five years younger than Samuel. Samuel is one year older than Judy. Is Judy younger or older than Ella?

____ (a) Who *are* these people, anyway?

____ (b) Who cares?

____ (c) Judy looks younger than Ella thanks to Samuel, who is actually her plastic surgeon. You, too, can look years younger. Just call Dr. Sam at 1-800-LIFT-MY-FACE and have your own free personal consultation.

6. Farmer Brown owns ten pigs. Three of them are brown, four of them are black, two of them are pink, and one of them is white. How many of the ten can say they are the same color as another of Farmer Brown's pigs?

____ (a) None of them can say because

____ (b) pigs can't

____ (c) talk

____ (d) did you really fall for the oldest trick in the book?

____ (e) all of the above

Scoring

5–6 Correct:	Win three days in New York City!
3–4 Correct:	Win a week in New York City!
0–2 Correct:	Win ten days in New York City!

Number Series Completion

Most intelligent people can recognize simple patterns in series of numbers. For example, anyone knows what the next number in this series must be: 10 20 30 40 _____.

Of course, it's...it's...it's...well, it's obvious that we're not just anyone, isn't it!

Directions

Study each number series below. Identify the pattern and fill in the missing number.

1. 11 30 12 30 1 30 2 30 _____
2. 200 150 100 _____
3. 2 2 _____
4. 99 86 32 _____
5. 2 4 6 8 _____
6. 1 800 _____

Number Series Completion Answers

1. 1 30 2 30
   2:30? Time to call the dentist!

2. 150 100
   50—your likely I.Q. after completing this book!

3. 2 2 *twain!*

4. 99 86 32 *hike!*

5. 2 4 6 8 *who do we appreciate?*

6. 1 800 *NO-BRAIN (our self-help support group hotline number!)*

Basic Operations Test

Follow the directions on this page. Using two #2 pencils or one #4 pencil or half a #8 pencil with a sharp point, fill in the bubbles on the answer sheet on the next page. You have exactly ten minutes to complete this test. 1, 2, 3, GO!

1. Fill in all bubbles beginning with the number 6.

2. Fill in all bubbles beginning with the number 1.

3. Fill in all bubbles with digits that, when added together, produce a sum of 9.

4. Erase anything that looks messy or smudged.

5. Chew on your pencil while waiting for your teacher to call time.

6. Put your head down on your desk while waiting for your teacher to call time.

7. Check to see if your teacher is still breathing.

8. In case of emergency, dial 911. Speak clearly to the operator who answers the phone. Be sure to give your address accurately.

```
ⒶⒷⒸⒹ  ⒶⒷⒸⒹ  ⒶⒷⒸⒹ  ⒶⒷⒸⒹ  ⒶⒷⒸⒹ
ⒶⒷⒸⒹ  ⒶⒷⒸⒹ  ⒶⒷⒸⒹ  ⒶⒷⒸⒹ  ⒶⒷⒸⒹ
ⒶⒷⒸⒹ  ⒶⒷⒸⒹ  ⒶⒷⒸⒹ  ⒶⒷⒸⒹ  ⒶⒷⒸⒹ
ⒶⒷⒸⒹ  ⒶⒷⒸⒹ  ⒶⒷⒸⒹ  ⒶⒷⒸⒹ  ⒶⒷⒸⒹ
ⒶⒷⒸⒹ  ⒶⒷⒸⒹ  ⑥①⑤①⑧①①①  ⒶⒷⒸⒹ  ⒶⒷⒸⒹ
ⒶⒷⒸⒹ  ⒶⒷⒸ㉚  ⒶⒷⒸⒹ  ㉗ⒷⒸⒹ  ⒶⒷⒸⒹ
ⒶⒷⒸⒹ  ⒶⒷ⑬Ⓓ  ⒶⒷⒸⒹ  Ⓐ⑭ⒸⒹ  ⒶⒷⒸⒹ
ⒶⒷⒸⒹ  Ⓐ㊁ⒸⒹ  ⒶⒷⒸⒹ  ⒶⒷ㊄Ⓓ  ⒶⒷⒸⒹ
ⒶⒷⒸⒹ  Ⓐ㊌ⒸⒹ  ⒶⒷⒸⒹ  ⒶⒷ㊅Ⓓ  ⒶⒷⒸⒹ
ⒶⒷⒸⒹ  ⑲ⒷⒸⒹ  ⒶⒷⒸⒹ  ⒶⒷⒸ⑰  ⒶⒷⒸⒹ
ⒶⒷⒸ㊒  ⒶⒷⒸ㊐  ㊀ⒷⒸ⑮  ㊅ⒷⒸⒹ  ㉞ⒷⒸⒹ
ⒶⒷⒸ⑪  ⒶⒷⒸ⑱  ⑲ⒷⒸ⑱  ㊁ⒷⒸⒹ  ⑲ⒷⒸⒹ
ⒶⒷⒸ㊅  ㊂ⒷⒸⒹ  ⒶⒷⒸⒹ  ⒶⒷⒸ㊅  ㊌ⒷⒸⒹ
ⒶⒷⒸⒹ  Ⓐ㉗ⒸⒹ  ⒶⒷⒸⒹ  ⒶⒷ⑯Ⓓ  ⒶⒷⒸⒹ
ⒶⒷⒸⒹ  Ⓐ⑱ⒸⒹ  ⒶⒷⒸⒹ  ⒶⒷ⑪Ⓓ  ⒶⒷⒸⒹ
ⒶⒷⒸⒹ  Ⓐ㊅ⒸⒹ  ⒶⒷⒸⒹ  ⒶⒷ㊅Ⓓ  ⒶⒷⒸⒹ
ⒶⒷⒸⒹ  Ⓐ⑬ⒸⒹ  ㊅ⒷⒸ⑬  ⒶⒷ㊁Ⓓ  ⒶⒷⒸⒹ
ⒶⒷⒸⒹ  Ⓐ㊄ⒸⒹ  Ⓐ⑭㊁Ⓓ  ⒶⒷ⑱Ⓓ  ⒶⒷⒸⒹ
ⒶⒷⒸⒹ  ⒶⒷ⑯Ⓓ  ⒶⒷⒸⒹ  Ⓐ⑮ⒸⒹ  ⒶⒷⒸⒹ
ⒶⒷⒸⒹ  ⒶⒷⒸ㊁  ⒶⒷⒸⒹ  ㊅ⒷⒸⒹ  ⒶⒷⒸⒹ
ⒶⒷⒸⒹ  ⒶⒷⒸⒹ  ㊅⑭㊒⑲  ⒶⒷⒸⒹ  ⒶⒷⒸⒹ
ⒶⒷⒸⒹ  ⒶⒷⒸⒹ  ⒶⒷⒸⒹ  ⒶⒷⒸⒹ  ⒶⒷⒸⒹ
ⒶⒷⒸⒹ  ⒶⒷⒸⒹ  ⒶⒷⒸⒹ  ⒶⒷⒸⒹ  ⒶⒷⒸⒹ
ⒶⒷⒸⒹ  ⒶⒷⒸⒹ  ⒶⒷⒸⒹ  ⒶⒷⒸⒹ  ⒶⒷⒸⒹ
ⒶⒷⒸⒹ  ⒶⒷⒸⒹ  ⒶⒷⒸⒹ  ⒶⒷⒸⒹ  ⒶⒷⒸⒹ
ⒶⒷⒸⒹ  ⒶⒷⒸⒹ  ⒶⒷⒸⒹ  ⒶⒷⒸⒹ  ⒶⒷⒸⒹ
ⒶⒷⒸⒹ  ⒶⒷⒸⒹ  ⒶⒷⒸⒹ  ⒶⒷⒸⒹ  ⒶⒷⒸⒹ
ⒶⒷⒸⒹ  ⒶⒷⒸⒹ  ⒶⒷⒸⒹ  ⒶⒷⒸⒹ  ⒶⒷⒸⒹ
ⒶⒷⒸⒹ  ⒶⒷⒸⒹ  ⒶⒷⒸⒹ  ⒶⒷⒸⒹ  ⒶⒷⒸⒹ
ⒶⒷⒸⒹ  ⒶⒷⒸⒹ  ⒶⒷⒸⒹ  ⒶⒷⒸⒹ  ⒶⒷⒸⒹ
```

Math Myths: True or False

•••

Directions

Write a T for *true* or an F for *false* in front of each question below.

1. ____ The number 2 hits it lucky in Las Vegas more often than the number six.

(True! Scientists have discovered that dust particles, flakes of human skin, mouse droppings, and other hard-to-see bits of dirt collect in the little indentations on dice spots. Thus, the side with the most spots—six—is more disgusting and weighs more than the other sides of the die with fewer spots, and, obviously, the lighter sides of the die will end up facing up most often.)

2. ____ If Elvis had lived until today, he would have drunk 67,093 diet Pepsi's.

(Again, true! The odd thing is that he never drank a single can of this particular soft drink during his lifetime.)

3. ____ Snow White really kept house for only six dwarfs.

(False. Ha! We caught you on this one!)

4. ____ Cher's tattoos cover just two percent of the entire surface of her skin.

(False again! Actually, it is just the reverse: Doctors have determined that only two percent of her skin can be considered a tattoo-free zone.)

5. ____ The number nine is just amazing!

(True! I mean, isn't it amazing that nine also means "no" in the German language, even if it is spelled differently?)

6. ____ The number four is just amazing!

(False. Actually, four is a very ordinary number.)

Math Magic

By now, your brain is probably almost totally busted from working so hard on all these math pages. We thought you might want a break at this point to learn a little numbers trick that will dazzle your friends. What's that you say? You don't have any friends now that you've been seen in public with a copy of this book? Okay, then, maybe you should try out this trick on somebody who *has* to talk to you, like your mother, or your teacher—or better yet, your guidance counselor.

1. Tell a friend you can guess his or her age. If your friend claims you already know his or her age, say, "Yeah, but I forgot what it is." If they know you at *all*, they'll believe you.

2. Tell your friend to write down the year of his or her birth. If your friend claims you can easily figure out his or her age from this, say, "No, I can't." If they know you at *all*, they'll believe you.

3. Say, "Subtract the number three from that date."

4. Say, "Add your age to that number." (If your friend is a dog, tell him or her to multiply by seven.)

5. Say, "Add six."

6. Say, "Multiply the whole amount by itself. Then divide it by your age *if* you had a birthday last year. Repeat this. Do it again. And again. And again."

7. Whoa! Even if your friend is weird enough to have stuck around doing all this arithmetic, who are we kidding here? No *way* is this going to work! You'd better start looking for a graceful way to bail out.

(If you can't think of one, here's the one we always use: Say, "I've got it! You are _____ (say your friend's age here) years old!" If you really didn't know your friend's age when you started this stupid trick, just guess—for friends, guess at least one year older to flatter them. For parents, teachers, and guidance counselors, guess a couple years younger—for the same reason.)

8. To avoid making gross mathematical errors in the future, tear this page out of your book.

Geometric Shape Identification

How adept are you at identifying shapes? In other words, are your perceptual skills in good "shape"? (Award yourself six I.Q. points for recognizing a pun.)

Directions
Put a check next to the correct name for each one of these shapes.

1.

_____(a) A piece of pizza, plus the extra one you stole from your little sister.

_____(b) An extra-large-size dunce cap for a fathead.

_____(c) An overweight triangle.

_____(d) A circle that was in a *baaad* accident.

2.

____(a) Your watch—right after you stepped on it.

____(b) A snake that just ate a stop sign.

____(c) A stop sign that just ate a snake.

____(d) A wolf in shape's clothing.

3.

____(a) An out-of-shape shape.

____(b) A bookworm that got squashed inside a novel.

____(c) Who knows? But we just saw it crawling up the back of your neck!

____(d) This book—after it's been in the garbage can for a week.

Geometric Perception

Carefully study this picture of two triangles. Which one of them *appears* to be larger?

The answer to this question can be found at the bottom of the page. (HINT: It's easier to turn the book upside down than it is to stand on your head to read the answer.)

A. **B.**

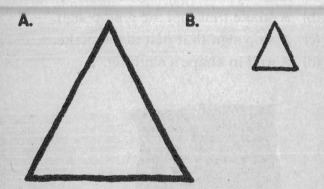

You're kidding! You actually *looked* at the answer to this one? Quick! Turn your book back right side up before anyone notices!

Mathematical
Patterns and Series

Study the series of full and empty glasses below. Can you, by *moving only one glass*, rearrange the glasses so that the pattern becomes, empty glass/full glass/empty glass/full glass/empty glass? The answer is on the next page.

Answer: Note that this graduate of

Brain Builders
...NOT!

did not even have to move *one single glass* to accomplish his idea of the pattern rearrangement. All he needed was our fabulous course...and his trusty straw.

Diagrammatic Representation Test

1. Which figure does not belong in this set?

(a)   (b)   (c)   (d)   (e)

[If you said figure (e) you are correct; figures (a), (b), and (c) are all walking *toward* the giant chicken, while figure (d) is walking *away*.

2. Which figure continues the sequence?

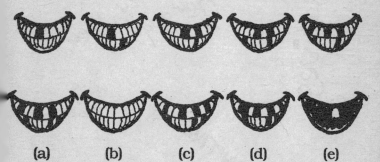

(a)   (b)   (c)   (d)   (e)

[If you said figure (b) you are correct. Obviously the person visited the dentist and, at great expense, had all his teeth capped.]

Capitalization Can Be Our Friend

bite
bit
bitten

Verbal
Skills
Section

sit
or
set?

using
double negatives

I, you, he, she,
it, we, they, them,
us, you guys

arise
arose
arisen

NEVER SPLIT INFINITIVES

Commas
and how to
use them

Reading Comprehension

Directions

As you read each paragraph below, try to concentrate on finding the main idea. If you can concentrate on more than one thing at a time, also concentrate on not falling off your chair. Put an X next to each correct answer. (You already know how to make an "X"—it's how you usually sign your name!)

1. Friction is the resistance created when one material moves against another. Many things people do would not be possible without friction. Our feet, for instance, would not grip the ground without friction. Belts would fall off machines. Screws would not stay in place.

The main idea of this paragraph is:

____(a) Friction is more interesting to read than nonfriction.

____(b) Friction is *soooo* boring.

____(c) It's time for lunch.

2. People have been mining for silver for hundreds of years. European royalty used silver for their wealth. The crowned head of Spain was thrilled about the discovery of Mexican and Peruvian silver mines. For 250 years, the mines at Potosí made millions of dollars for the Spanish kings.

The main idea of this paragraph is:

____(a) If you get a sliver in your finger, you can dig it out with a clean needle.

____(b) Spain was ruled by some kind of disgusting disembodied head.

____(c) Did somebody mention lunch?

3. No one knows for sure why the Leaning Tower of Pisa leans. It may be because its foundations were laid in sand. But after the first three stories were constructed, the tower slowly began to lean more and more. In the last one hundred years, it has leaned another foot. Engineers believe it might eventually fall right over!

The main idea of this paragraph is:

____(a) No way are you ever going up in that tower!

____(b) The Leaning Tower of Pisa has an extra foot. But the important question is, did it start out with two feet in the first place?

____(c) Did someone mention pizza? Let's send out!

4. You have probably eaten tapioca many times without realizing what it really is. Did you know it's actually made from the roots of the cassava plant? The roots are washed, peeled, and then soaked for four days. Then they are grated. The grated root is mixed with clean water. The dirt rises to the top and the starch settles on the bottom.

The main idea of this paragraph is:

____(a) You never really liked tapioca before, but now...

____(b) You'll get sick if you even see somebody *else* eating it!

____(c) Oh, great. Now nobody even *wants* lunch!

Vocabulary

....

Directions

Underline (that is, draw a line under) the two words in each sequence that you believe to be the closest in meaning (that is, that say about the same thing). The answers (that is, the part that tells you what's right) are under each question.

Example:

flyswatter spatula baseball bat coat hanger

(*Flyswatter* and *baseball bat*—because they're both used for swatting flies!)

1. karate squash banana judo

(*Karate* and *squash*—because they're both vegetables.)

2. crabgrass hay toenails three feet

(*Crabgrass* and *three feet*—because they both equal a yard.)

3. jogging running red goofball

(*Running* and *red*—because they both describe your nose!)

4. necks throats first skull

(*First* and *necks*—because they both
describe order, as in: "Are you *first* in the
line, or are you the *necks* one after that?")

5. Kenya please no way way

(*Kenya* and *please*—because they're both
requests, as in: "*Please* get your foot offa
my foot, for crying out loud!" and "*Kenya*
get your foot offa my foot, for crying out
loud?")

6. authors deadbeats duh cretins

(We refuse to answer this one on the
grounds we might incram...incrum...
uncrimpinate...er, on the grounds we
might get ourselves into trouble!)

Word-and-Phrase-Completion Test

....

Directions

All of the words, phrases, or names in the exercises below suggest an expression with the word *block* in it. Can you fill them all in? If you need help, choose from the *block* of words at the bottom of the next page. (We've put them in order so even a blockhead could figure them out!)

1. A kind of juice made from blocks:
   BLOCK ___ ___ ___

2. What your friends *think* they are, but what only *you* really are:

   ___ ___ ___ ___ ___ ___ ___ ___ ___
   ___ ___ ___ BLOCK

3. A famous book about a horse:
   BLOCK ___ ___ ___ ___ ___ ___

4. What you might *like* to do to writers of I.Q. puzzles and tests:

__ __ __ __ __ __ __ __ __ __

BLOCKS __ __ __

5. A fancy kind of running shoe:
REE __ __ __ __ __ __

6. What you're probably experiencing while trying to figure out these answers:
__ __ __ __ __ __ BLOCK

Block of Answers

Blockade

Cool Kid on the Block

Block Beauty

Knock Their Blocks Off

Reeblocks

Mental Block

Just One More Reading Comprehension Test

....

Directions

Read the following paragraph. Then answer all the questions about it.

Sally Jane woke up. She was very happy. It was her birthday. She hoped to get many presents. She especially wanted Little Frizzy Curling Iron to make little curls all over her head. So when her big brother, Max, who had never remembered her birthday before in his life, surprised her by giving her the Little Frizzy Curling Iron, she was overjoyed. Sally Jane ran up to her room and plugged in her gift. When the light blinked off, Sally Jane took a large piece of her long blonde hair and twirled it into the curling iron. It was not until she smelled the funny smell that she knew something was very wrong. She looked in the mirror at her *singed* hair. "Max," she said through her teeth, "would you please come up here?"

1. The best title for this story is:

(a) Sally Jane and Her Birthday Boo-Boo

(b) Sally Jane's Evil Brother

(c) Bald Is Beautiful

2. The word *singed* in the second to last sentence means:

(a) to have sung

(b) yellow

(c) charred like a shrimp on the barbie

3. How do you think the authors of this paragraph felt while writing about Sally Jane?

(a) deeply disturbed

(b) like laughing hysterically

(c) unsure whether their editor would print such drivel

4. The main idea expressed in this paragraph is:

(a) Sally Jane was greedy and got what she deserved.

(b) Sally Jane's brother needs professional help.

(c) Always read the directions when you get a curling iron for your birthday.

Verbal Completion Test

....

Directions

Look at the old doohickeys below. Think about how each whatsit might best be completed. Then pick the best thingamajig that completes each whachamacallit.

1. An apple a day keeps the doctor...

(a) in the orchard

(b) on *General Hospital*

(c) chewing

2. A stitch in time saves...

(a) thread

(b) your clock

(c) the seat of your pants

3. A friend in need is a friend...

(a) to the end

(b) of a dog

(c) like me

4. Actions speak louder than...

(a) my teacher

(b) fractions

(c) my dentist

Son of Vocabulary

Directions

Match the word with the sentence in which it is used. If you miss any of these questions, see your doctor today!

Words:

(a) deceit

(b) falsify

(c) insulate

(d) burden

(e) ammonia

Sentences:

_____ I waited up till midnight, but you got insulate I didn't see you.

_____ Those sneakers are great, but have you tried ammonia to see if they fit?

_____ I have two pockets on deceit on my new jeans.

_____ My uncle Ray went goose hunting, but there wasn't a burden sight, so he came home empty-handed.

_____ I can stand with a book on my head, but it falsify try to walk.

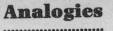

Analogies

••••••••••••••••••••••••••

This is a series of questions designed to test your innate ability to visualize significant relationships between selected items from our lexicon. If you finished reading that last sentence, give yourself ten bonus I.Q. points. If you understood even a single word of it, you can skip high school.

Example: SLEEP is to BED as STUDY is to:

(a) MALL

(b) YAWN

(c) GET REAL

Answer: (a) because a BED is a *place* where you SLEEP, and the MALL is the *place* where you STUDY the latest fashion trends.

1. COMPUTER is to MACHINE as YOUR BRAIN is to:

(a) BED

(b) A BEAN BURRITO

(c) THERE'S ABSOLUTELY NO COMPARISON BETWEEN YOUR BRAIN AND A COMPUTER

3. IDIOTIC is to DUMMY as STUPID is to:

(a) THIS BOOK

(b) THIS BOOK

(c) ALL THREE OF THE ABOVE

3. ROSE is to FLOWER as THISTLE is to:

(a) THAT'LL

(b) WHISTLE

(c) GET REAL

4. FOLLOW-UP is to PREPARATION as AFTER-MATH is to:

(a) BEFORE MATH

(b) DUNNO

(c) AFTER LUNCH

5. FAT is to THIN as INTELLIGENCE is to:

(a) WART HOG

(b) PLAIN OLD HOG

(c) RAZORBACK HOG

Analogy Answer Scale

4–5 Correct:	Seek immediate professional help.
3–4 Correct:	Ditto.
1–2 Correct:	Dotto.
0 Correct:	Dutto.

Verbal Memory Test

Most of us can remember our first names. Maybe even our last names. But what about those tricky middle names? Can we all remember them, hmmm? We don't think so, or our names aren't...uh...um...well, if you really care, you can look on the cover of this book.

How many of the middle names of the famous personalities and/or things listed below can you remember? Fill in the blanks. The answers are...well, to be honest, *somebody's* writing partner lost the answers—*again!*

1. Winnie _____ Pooh

2. Smokey _____ Bear

3. Fruit _____ the Loom

4. The Queen _____ England
   (Watch out! This one's tricky!)

5. Oscar _____ Grouch

6. Cher

7. Cream _____ Wheat

8. Attila _____ Hun

9. Calvin _____ Hobbes

10. Guns _____ Roses

Matching Words Test

•••

Directions

Match the word or phrase in Column A with the word or phrase in Column B that you think makes the prettiest pattern of straight lines on this page.

Column A	Column B
Saturn's Rings	Onion Rings
Totally Tubular	MTV
Barbie's Dream House	Liz Taylor's Rings
Dave Letterman	Mallomar Breath
Chicken Pox	Bathtub Rings
Betty and Veronica	*The Cucumber That Ate Chicago*
Crash Dummy	Dill Pickle
Rabbit Ears	Hurl Chunks
Blowfish	Nose Rings

Word Maze

....

The letters in the box below probably look like a scrambled mess to you. (Well, to be honest, if we've done our job with this book, probably *all* letters look like a scrambled mess to you by now!) But, if you study them carefully, some words will start to emerge. When you find a word, write it on a sheet of notebook paper. When you're finished, a message will be revealed to you. The answer appears at the bottom of the page.

```
H E L P I A M T R A
P P E D I N S I D E
T H I S S T U P I D
B O O K ! P L E A S
E G E T M E O U T !
I A M D E S P E R A
T E ! ! ! ! ! ! ! !
```

Answer

THIS IS THE FINEST, MOST EDUCATIONAL BOOK I HAVE EVER READ. I SURELY HOPE THAT THERE WILL BE A SEQUEL.

Grandson of Vocabulary

Directions

Here we go again. Match each word with the sentence in which it is used. If you miss any of these questions, you are required to buy a second copy of

Brain Builders
...NOT!

Words:

(a) aardvark   (b) botany   (c) forfeit

(d) malicious   (e) soda

Sentences:

____ My mother wondered whether you had botany good tomatoes at this market.

____ When any war begins, the malicious called out.

____ Doing math problems is aardvark, but it pays off on the tests.

____ A horse has forfeit, while a human walks on only two.

____ She poured all of her guests more ginger ale soda party would last a little longer.

what do they mean here

Huh?

**Some
Other
Stuff
Skills
Section**

My pencil broke.

How do we know what to do?

How much time do we have?

What if I don't know my zip code?

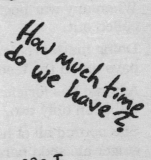

can I be excused?

Practical Intelligence

••

Okay, maybe you know that 34X + 4Y − 55Z = 23% off retail, but do you look both ways before you cross the street?

The following questions have been scientifically designed to measure your practical intelligence—intelligence that simply cannot be located with ordinary vocabulary quizzes and math tests, like the ones your teachers give in school.

In this test, you must put yourself in each of the situations and decide what to do.

Practical Intelligence Test

....

1. You walk into math class and suddenly remember: You *did* have homework last night! *Ohmygosh*, you think to yourself as all the rest of your goody-goody little class-mates get out their notebooks and start putting their papers on your teacher's desk, *now what do I do?*

(a) Offer to hand in your friend's paper, erase your friend's—make that ex-friend's—name, write your own name in its place, and hand it in.

(b) Fall to the ground, writhing pitifully, and get sent to the nurse's office.

(c) Walk up to your teacher's desk, explain that you simply forgot to do the assign-ment, that you will do it tonight, plus all the extra-credit problems, and that you promise never to let this happen again. (As you do this, slip a note into your teacher's hand in which you promise to rake leaves in your teacher's yard, walk his dog, and clean out his gutters.)

2. Your neighbor, Mr. Jones, asks you to water his plants while he is on vacation, and he pays you fifteen dollars in advance. You happily take the money and hit the video arcade. Two weeks pass. Then one day the doorbell rings, and there stands Mr. Jones holding a flowerpot with something brown drooping from it. *Yikes!* you think. *I forgot to water those plants! Now what do I do?*

(a) Explain to Mr. Jones that you wanted to water his plants but that aliens came into your room and tied you up, and you just escaped five minutes ago and were on your way over to see about his plants.

(b) Tell Mr. Jones about the water shortage that occurred while he was away and about the announcement on TV that no one was to use even one drop of water for anything but extreme emergency purposes, such as washing your car before a big date.

(c) Tell Mr. Jones the truth. Right!

3. You have a crush on Sara Smith, a new girl in your class, and when she shyly asks if you'd like to come to her house for dinner, you are beside yourself with joy. When you sit down with Sara and her family, you say, "Wow, all this stuff looks really different from the pizza we have for dinner every night." "Yes," replies Sara, "we know that in the future, everyone will eat insects as a good source of protein." That's when you notice that everything on your plate has little legs and eyeballs and antennae. *Whoa,* you think, as Sara and the rest of her family start crunching away, *what do I do now?*

(a) Explain that you've had to stop eating roasted roach because of your allergies.

(b) Excuse yourself to wash your hands and let yourself out of the house.

(c) Tell Sara the truth: that you think eating insects is nauseating. If she doesn't believe you, take one bite and let her watch as the contents of your stomach appear on her dining room table!

Answers

In each case, the answer is, once again, (d): Become a hermit and you'll never have to deal with these stupid situations.

Matching Methods

The heads below have been separated from their bodies. (Gross! what is this, *Friday the 13th, Part 27* ???)

However, if you look carefully, you can identify certain clues that will tell you which head goes with which body. Draw a line from each head to the body on which is belongs. Turn the page to find the answers.

Answers

What? You're saying this *isn't* how *you* would have orga-
nized the heads? Well, it just so happens that we wrote the
book, and we say this is the answer. Go write a book of
your own.

Self-Imaging

The ability to see yourself as others see you is an important, though often overlooked, aspect of intelligence. The following exercise has been designed to help you see, in your mind's eye, an accurate picture of yourself.

1. Close your eyes.

2. Think about what you are doing at this very moment—reading a book that will help you to boost your intelligence.

3. Keep your thoughts in the present moment. Do not let your mind drift to the repulsive meat loaf that they served today in the school cafeteria or to the fact that the girl who sits in front of you in math class has not washed the back of her neck in a long time.

4. Repeat this calming phrase: I am taking an intelligence test, I am taking an intelligence test, I am taking an intelligence test.

5. In your mind, picture yourself taking the intelligence test.

6. Now, turn the page to see whether your mental image accurately reflects the way others see you.

Does your image of yourself fit with the way others see you?

Comparisons

The ability to tell whether things are *alike* or *different* is a sign of intelligence. Take this test. Afterward, see if you feel more *alike* than you did before you took the test, or more *different* from the way you felt after the test.

1. Which is least like the other three?

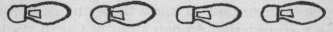

2. Which is more alike than the above?

3. Circle the one that is most alike. Underline the one that is most different.

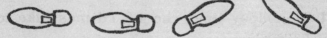

4. Pick the one that is most *alike* and most *different*, while at the same time, being the most fashionable.

Caution: Check your answers to make *shoe* you have made the correct response.

What? Another Aptitude Test?

After you have completed some of the *Brain Builders*, testing your aptitude again is important. Such a test can tell you if you have changed from the experience. Such a test can make you aware of what kinds of things you are now attracted to and what things still make you want to hurl. It is especially important to know these things if you are considering dropping out of fourth grade to get a job.

Directions

For each series of questions, circle the answer that most appeals to the real you.

1. At holiday time, the gift I'd most like to have is:

(a) Barbie's Dream Pro Wrestler Date

(b) Junior Bungee Jumping Kit

(c) Pierce 'em Yourself Ear Decorating Kit (comes complete with earrings, ice pick, cotton balls, bandages, and emergency telephone numbers)

(d) Barbie's Dream Vacuum with Attachments

2. If I have an hour to myself, I most like to:

(a) watch the daytime soaps

(b) practice hang gliding from my garage roof

(c) read a great book like *101 Cat and Dog Jokes* or any of the other hilarious titles by the Riddle Czarinas Lisa Eisenberg and Katy Hall

(d) take out the garbage

3. If I had a pet, I'd choose a:

(a) furry, little cutsie puppy

(b) full-grown attack Doberman

(c) piranha

(d) Chia pet

4. If I were to pick out something for myself that had feathers, it would be:

(a) a six-foot boa

(b) a parrot

(c) Big Bird

(d) a feather duster

5. When I turn on the radio, I most often listen to:

(a) the sound of my own breathing

(b) anything by the Bone Crushers

(c) static

(d) peppy songs to make me work even faster

Aptitude Analysis

If most of your answers were (a), you are a romantic individual. The type of work that would most likely appeal to you is: none. Our advice is: Marry rich.

If most of your answers were (b), you like to live on the edge. Alpine downhill skiing, scuba diving in shark-infested waters, parachuting over the North Pole—you're in for a life of adventure. Our advice: Tell your loved ones to look into big insurance policies.

If you picked the (c) answers, you probably already know you're in bad shape. In a word: sick. You'll never hold down a job, but don't give up hope. It's people like you who keep those hideous daytime talk shows in business. Our advice: Get an agent and get booked on *Oprah Winfrey* or *Sally Jesse Raphael.*

If you picked (d), you like to keep things neat and tidy, shiny and clean. You will never be out of work. By the way, can you be at our apartment next Thursday at 10:00 A.M.? And do you do windows?

Take Another Break!

Boy, have you sweated over these quizzes. Now it's time to give that old thinker of yours a rest. Just follow these simple instructions, and the strain of your brain will go down the drain!

Relaxation Exercise #1

1. Close your eyes.

2. Open your mouth slightly.

3. Do not move.

4. Stay like this until someone comes into the room and comments on the lifelike piece of sculpture.

Relaxation Exercise #2

1. Lie down on the floor.

2. Raise your legs in the air, bending your knees.

3. Hold your hands just above your chest, elbows bent.

4. Let your tongue loll out of your mouth.

5. Stare at the ceiling.

6. Stay like this until someone comes into the room and rubs your tummy, saying, "Good doggie!"

Missing Details Test

The illustrations below are complete...*not!*

One small but essential detail is missing from each drawing. Can you find it? The missing details have been filled in on the next page. Can you find *that*?

Memory Test

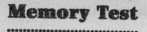

Just how good is your memory? Study the picture below for three solid minutes. Then turn the page and see how many of the questions you can answer.

Memory Test Questions

1. Just who does that dude on the bike think he is, anyway? _____

2. Does he think he's too cool to live, or what? _____

3. What is the girl in the window's middle name? _____

4. What color is her headband? _____

5. Why has she been grounded for the last three weeks? _____

6. How did she manage to sneak out of the house? _____

7. Why do you suppose her parents are just so...well, like, totally, hopelessly unfair? _____

8. How much do you think she paid for her shoes? _____

9. What day of the week is it? _____

10. How do you spell "obfuscation"? _____

11. Do you think the illustrator who drew this picture was in a bad mood when he drew it, or what? _____

Classification

••••••••••••••••••••••••••••••••••

In each problem, circle the word or phrase that does NOT belong with the others.

Example: mitten, scarf, coat, hat, fudge

Answer: *mitten,* because it is the only thing you would have to take off if you didn't want to get wool on your fudge

1. rat, hat, you, bat, cat, gerbil
2. first base, second base, have, third base
3. gooey, slimy, to, ucky, sticky, icky, gummy
4. take, car, Irish setter, truck, limo, taxi
5. Louise, Lulu, lessons, Lisa, Butch, Linda
6. football, to, baseball, basketball, eyeball
7. pickle, giggle, get, laugh, guffaw, chortle
8. a score this rotten, toe, elbow

Correct Answers

1. you 2. have 3. to 4. take 5. lessons 6. to 7. get
   8. a score this rotten
   8 Correct: Try again.
   6–7 Correct: Better luck next time.
   3–5 Correct: Not Bad!
   0–2 Correct: Excellent!

Memory and Creative Intelligence

•••••••••••••••••••••••••••••••

The pictures on this page and the next page may look the same to you. (If they do, make an appointment with your eye specialist today!) But actually, seven small but significant details have been changed from one picture to the next. Study both pictures and try to find all seven changes. After you have found the changes, see if you can use your creative intelligence to explain *how* the changes may have come about. Then turn the page to see how many you got right.

Picture One

Picture Two

Memory and Creative Intelligence Answers

The following details have changed between Picture One and Picture Two:

1. The boy, whose name is Durwood, has put on his old Halloween chicken suit.

2. Durwood is leaning back in his chair, because it is a more comfortable position for him in his chicken suit.

3. Since it is seven o'clock, Durwood has abandoned his homework to tune in to his favorite radio station, WHO-U, which is featuring a Frankie Avalon festival.

4. Durwood's friend Filbert has come over, bringing with him the large anchovy-broccoli pizza, the favorite of both boys.

5. Filbert, not to be outdone by his buddy Durwood, is wearing his Halloween costume, from the year he went trick-or-treating as a wild boar.

6. Five minutes have elapsed between Picture one and Picture Two.

Finding Details In Pictures

Directions

There are five things in this picture beginning with the letter I. Can you find them all? Can you find just one? The answers are upside down at the bottom of the page.

Logic Problem

....

Imagine that you're in a land called Hallberg where half the people wear White Hats and half the people wear Brown Hats. On Saturdays, the White Hats always walk on the right side of the street, and they always tell lies. On Sundays, the Brown Hats always walk on the left side of the street, and always tell the truth. (What do they do on Monday, Tuesday, Wednesday, Thursday, and Friday? They don't have the strength to do anything then, because those are the *weak*-days!)

Okay, okay, anyway, say you're walking down the street in Hallberg one Saturday, and you see a White Hat. The White Hat calls to you from the left side of the street and says, "I am wearing a Brown Hat, and I am telling you a lie when I say this." At the very same instant, a Brown Hat calls to you from the other side of the street, and says, "I am wearing a Brown Hat, and I am telling you the truth when I say this." Which hat is really telling the truth?

Huh? What is the correct answer? See the next page.

Actually, there are several correct answers to this Logic Puzzle. Here are some possibilities:

1. You say, "Don't you know I can't possibly understand you if you both talk at once? Didn't anyone ever teach you people to take turns? Sheesh!"

2. You say, "Brown or White, those are the ugliest hats I've ever seen. Honestly, I'm not telling a lie when I say this, and that's the truth!"

3. You say, "Who *cares* who's telling the truth or not? All *I* care about is getting out of this nightmare! Who ever heard of a dump named Hallberg, anyway?"

4. You say, "If a Brown Hat is calling me from one side of the street, and a White Hat is calling me from the other, that must mean that *I'm* in the middle of the street, and here comes a big diesel...... EEEEEYYYYAAAAIII!"

Connective Intelligence

••

Some things naturally go together. Ham and eggs. Two #2 pencils and standardized tests.

Other things, you have to work a little harder to see the connection. The Brady family and Concord grapes. (Both come in bunches.)

Now use your bunch o' brains to make the connections among the items listed below. Write your idea of how these things go together on the line. Compare your answers with those of your friends. Or enemies. Laugh a lot. Then look at the real answers on page 77.

1. (a) soft (b) pin (c) Lucille

(d) _____

2. (a) *Full House* (b) *Card Sharks* (c) *Flipper*

(d) _____

3. (a) South (b) North (c) vault

(d) _____

4. (a) sour cream (b) bean (c) sheep

(d) _____

5. (a) Bobby Bonilla (b) Darryl Strawberry

(c) Batman (d) _____

6. (a) *Diff'rent Strokes* (b) *A Different World*

(c) Different Channel

(d) _____

Connective Intelligence Answers

1. You can add *ball* to the end of each word. Or not.

2. Flipper's favorite poker hand *is* a full house. And talk about a card shark! If you're ever out swimming in the ocean and are approached by a dolphin who says, "How about a friendly little game?" watch out!

3. The meaning of each word can be changed significantly by the addition of the word *pole*.

4. Three kinds of dip, but we don't recommend serving (c) at parties.

5. Bobby and Darryl step up to the plate to bat, which makes them batmen, too.

6. If you cut school to watch (a) or (b), and your mom walks into the room, you'd better switch to a (c)—preferably educational TV.

Moral Intelligence

Sure you can solve difficult math problems, but does that make it *right*? Study the examples below. Write R on the line if you think this is the *right* thing to do. Write W if you think it is *wrong*. Write C if you think it is wrong but you'd do it anyway except that you're afraid you'll get *caught*.

_____ **1.** Ask your older brother to do your history report for you.

_____ **2.** Ask your younger brother to do your history report for you.

_____ **3.** Ask your teacher whether you really, really, really have to do a history report.

_____ **4.** Beg both your brothers and anyone else who walks into the room to do your history report for you.

_____ **5.** Offer cash to anyone willing to do your history report for you.

_____ **6.** The night before your history report is due, write it yourself.

____ 7. Get together with some friends. Call one of your other friends on the phone and in a high, squeaky voice, say, "Is Jacob there?" When the phone answerer says, "Sorry, you've got the wrong number," apologize and hang up. Repeat this a minimum of twelve times. Wait three minutes. Dial your friend's number again. In a low voice, say, "Hello, this is Jacob. Have there been any calls for me?"

____ 8. Buy one hundred copies of

Brain Builders

...NOT!

Donate them anonymously to your school library.

Stop!
this can't be true!

More stuff?

Some More Stuff and Then It's Over

you're kidding

You can't do this to us!

I thought the tests were over!

PLEASE, NO MORE!

I won't do any more

NO NO NO

not me

I.Q. Post-test

Wow! You actually made it to the end of this book. That is absolutely amaz...hello...are you there? We're talking to you. Yes, you with your mental muscles flexing inside that hard, bony skull of yours.

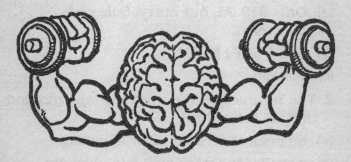

Hurts, doesn't it?

Well, the pain is almost over. All that's left for you to do is take the I.Q. Post-test. Score the test and compare this score with the score you got on the I.Q. Pre-test (see page 12) and you will see exactly how many points your I.Q. has gone up.

Directions

Answer these three questions. By analyzing your responses, amazingly enough, we will determine your *exact* I.Q.

1. Which of the following scientific formulas best describes the weight of gravity on a day in which the humidity is fourteen percent?

(a) Only $13.95, but hurry! Sale ends Saturday!

(b) U R A Q T I N V U

(c) Similac

2. The meaning of the word *vidaspecificaspatially* is defined as:

(a) an ancient term for a jar of pickles

(b) a really long word with lots of letters

(c) like a really cute word to use to impress your boyfriend's parents

3. What number can be doubled, resulting in an even number, tripled, resulting in an odd number, and quadrupled, resulting in a number so odd that no one has heard of it?

(a) 6

(b) six

(c) Could you repeat the question?

I.Q. Post-Test Analysis

Answers

1. The correct answer is (d).

2. Again, the correct answer is (d).

3. Here, the correct answer is, of course, (d).

I.Q. Scoring

You can score this test yourself by carefully following these directions: EXAMPLE:

1. Total the number of correct points you scored on the test.

   3

2. Multiply that by your shoe size.

   $3 \times 10\frac{1}{2}D = 31\frac{1}{2}$

3. Divide that by the number of toes on your left foot.

   $31\frac{1}{2} \div 2 = 15\frac{3}{4}$

4. Multiply that by your teacher's age.

   $15\frac{3}{4} \times 100 = 1575$

5. Divide that by the age your teacher claims to be.

   $1575 \div 10 =$

6. The result is your I.Q.:

   $157\frac{1}{2}$

I.Q. Chart

0–50	Very smart...for a jellyfish
50–75	Smarter than most people's dogs
76–100	More brain activity than the average microwave oven
100–130	Able to leap tall buildings at a single bound
130–140	You often amaze yourself
140–150	Warning! Touching your own forehead can result in a severe burn.
150+	You have been declared a national mental treasure. It is a waste of our country's most precious resource, namely, you, to do any activity that prevents you from doing the activities in

Brain Builders
...NOT!

full time. This includes taking out the garbage, cleaning the parakeet's cage, and clearing the table.

Show this one to your mom. If she buys it, then you've *more* than gotten your money's worth out of this little book.